Sportsviewers Guide
SKIING

Peter Bills

DAVID & CHARLES
Newton Abbot   London

Contents

David Vine

British Library Cataloguing in Publication Data
Bills, Peter
  Skiing. — (Sportsviewers guides)
  1. Skis and skiing — History
  I. Title II. Series
  796.93'09   GV854

  ISBN 0-7153-8505-4

The Sportsviewers' Guide to Skiing was produced and designed by Siron Publishing Limited of 20 Queen Anne Street, London W1, Series editor: Nicholas Keith Photographs by Tommy Hindley and Tony Henshaw of Professional Sport.

Typeset by ABM Typographics Ltd, Hull and printed by Printer Industria Gráfica SA Cuatro Caminos, Apartado 8, Sant Vicenç dels Horts, Barcelona, Spain DLB 17342-1983 for David & Charles (Publishers) Limited Brunel House Newton Abbot Devon

Foreword

There you are, sitting in your armchair in front of a blazing log fire on a winter's Sunday afternoon. Suddenly, to the music of 'Pop Looks Bach', you are transported to the sun, snow and the glamour of the mountains — and the glamour of what has now become one of the most dramatic and colourful sports in the world.

It's BBC's *Ski Sunday* and for the next 45 minutes or so it's my job to be your host, guide, commentator and interviewer on the latest round of the world cup's white circus, the world championships or the Olympic Games. 'It's all right for him' you're all saying, out there in all that lovely sun with all those lovely people, like a three-month holiday — and he gets paid for it.

Let me 'open the door' as it were to the back room, the part of the circus that, unless something goes drastically wrong, you never see or hear about. My producer and I have planned to arrive in the resort by Thursday at the latest, Wednesday afternoon if possible. Somewhere between London and Europe it's a fair bet that the weather, all sunny and lovely in the brochure, is going to be a mixture of pea soup, driving rain, a foot or two of slush or six feet and more of new snow. So the travel schedule goes out of the window but eventually you get there to find that the hotel is booked out, the kitchen staff have gone off and the bar has shut. Never mind — it's glamorous. They told you so.

In the morning it's off to the mountain to meet the stars. After a long walk, there it is, the mountain on which it will all happen — the start-hut a couple of miles away up in the trees and the clouds, the finish line just in front of where we're heading for — the line of commentary boxes already being taken over by 'the speakers' as they call them from all over the world. Inside the chicken coops there's a mass of cable, TV monitor screens (Hey Fritzi, mine's not working again . . .), head sets and microphones. From the window (anybody brought the Windowlene?) we can see the finish line and about 100 metres above it.

Yes, you're right. We never see the race! Our view is like yours at home on a TV screen, which is why, today, we are off up the mountain while the training is going on, checking the course, watching the practice runs, comparing the form and getting a mental picture of every turn, every bump, every camera angle.

Tomorrow on race day, we'll rely on the television director of the country we're in to bring us the right pictures as we commentate live, never knowing what he's going to show us next. That's another reason why tonight we'll be with as many teams as we can, picking up the odd bit of gossip and delighted to have found out that the man we've always recognised by his beard has shaved it off for a bet. Without that little snippet, it could have been a case of 'And there's . . . well, someone' when we're 'live' tomorrow.

By eight o'clock in the evening, the race office issues the most vital piece of paper yet — the start list, the numbers drawn by the racers and armed with that it's back to the hotel room and the coffee pot to start the ski commentator's nightmare, the preparation of something like 100 crib cards containing all the information you'll need for the race. You'll probably never have time to look at it, but somehow it sticks, hopefully not in your throat at just the wrong moment.

3

History and development

From earliest times in Scandinavia and Russia, skiing was (and still is today) regarded as much more than a sport; it was a practical and efficient means of transport across land which was covered in snow for much of the year. Man used skis to help feed himself and his family by hunting animals in the dense forests of the north.

It is much the same today for trappers, fishermen and hunters who work in the remote northern areas of Norway, Sweden, Finland and Russia. Skis are tools of man's most basic needs — far removed from winter sports on the elegant and fashionable pistes of the world.

Skis dating back to the Stone Age — 2500BC — have been found in peat bogs in Scandinavia. Roughly cut skis they may have been — more like basic wooden boards in essence — but they performed the same function as holiday-makers now require: that is to say they were means of transport across snow several feet deep. From those crude skis refinements soon followed. To hunt the animals — usually elk or reindeer — man needed equipment to get him across the snow as quickly as possible. Hence the gradual development of wooden boards which enabled greater speed.

The Chinese liked all kinds of games and sports and recognised the need for transport across land often made all but impassable by the elements. Chinese records mentioned skiing as far back as the seventh to tenth centuries. The recorders of events in the T'ang Dynasty wrote of their northern neighbours as 'Turks who ride horses of wood'.

In the eighth century, a Lombard writing in Latin talked of people 'hunting wild animals by leaping forward using contrivances of wood curved like a bow'. In England, a map dated 1280 shows a man on skis in Norway and a 'horse-footed' man in

Sir Henry Lunn

China.

Life in these parts of northern Europe demanded the use of the first 'skis' much more than in the areas of Europe which now are associated with skiing and racing. The geographical regions which today form Austria, Germany and France may have seen some kind of ski in use, but the mountains would not have been of vital importance to the everyday life of local inhabitants.

Snow-shoe shuffle, Indian-file in Canada (Mary Evans Picture Library).

Kitzbühel (photograph supplied by the Austrian tourist office (London).

People in Scandinavia and Russia had to cross the snowy wastes to find their food; people in central Europe did not need to cross the vast mountain ranges for such basic necessities. In fact, until the time of the Industrial Revolution in 18th and 19th century Britain, when roads and railways began to break out of the towns into the largely undeveloped countryside, workers often went to work on 'skees' in severe weather.

Even as the twenty-first century approaches, many people in lands such as Sweden and Norway use skis for everyday chores such as shopping or travelling to work. In those countries, although mountain ranges do exist, overland skiing is more customary. This method of skiing on the flat is known as *langlauf*. Long, gruelling *langlauf* races are held throughout the winter season in Scandinavia. Often up to thirty or fifty kilometres in distance, these races demand the ultimate in physical strength and stamina, allied to smooth use of the longer *langlauf* skis.

As society developed, the idea of using skis for other than practical purposes began to gain ground. After 1800, the idea of skiing for enjoyment began to flourish and it is from this time that the idea of ski-racing probably emerged.

Legend tells us that the people of Tsterdal, north of the Norwegian city we now call Oslo, found a man to play some tricks on small mountain slopes near his home. Then Norway produced a ski which stayed flat to the ground (unlike the *langlauf* kind which, even today, flap loose at the back to enable the ski to be moved and lifted easily off the ground. So skis could be used for jumping and faster downhill paths, and this eventually led to organised races.

It is said that the United States was introduced to the sport by Norwegians who crossed the Atlantic Ocean and the Americans soon followed Norway's lead in staging races. Canada, with its marvellous expanse of the Rocky Mountains in the west, was another centre of keen interest. As the idea attracted more enthusiasts, small ski clubs gradually formed around the world.

Organisation

One of the many considerable anomalies of skiing as a sport is that it was the British who introduced it to many parts of Europe, especially Switzerland. That a nation surrounded, dominated and influenced by mountains should need the British to produce the idea of ski-racing is hard to comprehend. However, it was an Englishman, Sir Arnold Lunn, who pioneered slalom racing in its modern sense after the First World War and his father, Henry, instigated the idea of skiing holidays at the turn of the century.

Races were staged in Switzerland in 1902 and clubs such as the Davos English ski club and the Ski Club of Great Britain were formed. Downhill racing was the first style introduced; slalom followed as an altogether different challenge. The mounting interest in all aspects and areas of skiing, made the need for an overall controlling body paramount. Thus, the Fédération Internationale de Ski (FIS) came into being in 1924 and that year the first international downhill and slalom racing was held. The downhill was held from Scheidegg to Grindelwald, the slalom at Mürren.

Arnold Lunn was one of the prime movers in the creation of organised skiing but other Britons were also closely involved. He devised the first modern slalom course at Mürren in 1922. Lord Roberts of Kandahar, for instance, put up a skiing cup, thus creating an event which remains today. The race is called the Arlberg-Kandahar, run at the resort of St Anton in the western Tyrol.

Downhill racing in Austria, the home of the modern downhill men, did not gain credence until 1929 when the country first staged national championships. The Swiss, French and Germans soon followed. The first winter Olympics were held in 1936.

In 1967, the World Alpine Ski Cup took shape, creating a continuous series of downhill and slalom races throughout the European countries. Races which had by then acquired great tradition — such as the Arlberg-Kandahar and the Hahnenkamm — were incorporated into this winter sports circuit.

Skiing has continued to develop in many ways from Lunn's great vision in the early part of this century, and from those first movements of hunting men on coarse lumps of wood, it has become a multi-million pound industry.

Founding father:
Sir Arnold Lunn, one of
the pioneers of ski racing,
photographed in
the 1920s.

Early racer: Cecil Hopkinson,
winner of a
race in 1911.

7

Rules

For the purposes of definition, it is simpler to partition each aspect of skiing than to describe various rules, regulations and terminology appropriate to the individual disciplines. There are five main sections: downhill, slalom, giant slalom, ski jumping and cross country *(langlauf)*. Biathlon is a sport which involves the use of skis together with the rifle for shooting tests but it comes outside the main field of skiing.

Downhill

Penalties are comparatively few on downhill racing. Competitors can be eliminated if they do not go through the gates on the course but, in normal circumstances, this presents little problem. No unauthorised help is allowed but skiers can finish without a ski-pole. It is permissable, too, to finish with only one ski.

The organisers must adhere to many more stringent conditions than the racers themselves. The committee must ensure that small objects are removed from the course and potential hazards are covered or blocked off from the racers' possible path by means of snow banks, straw and netting.

The starting order is determined by a draw, with the leading skiers in a group of fifteen. No nation is allowed more than four skiers in each of the first two groups. Previous results determine which skiers are put into the top fifteen and those in that group have the advantage because the piste is usually at peak condition after the first few runs.

It is normal for the first group of fifteen, therefore, to provide the eventual winner. But the 1982–3 winter season in Europe proved that it is still possible for racers outside that top group to come from the ranks to win. Peter Lüscher (Switzerland), Bruno Kernan (Switzerland) and Helmut Höflehner (Austria) did just that in various races that winter.

Electronic timing is used from the split-second when the racer leaves the hut at the top of the mountain, having been counted down from five. Normally, the poles are outside the hut on the first few centimetres of the run to allow the racer to push off. His body must be behind the line so that it sets off the time-clock as it passes through the barrier to begin the run. Re-runs are comparatively rare but can occur. If they do, for whatever reason, the time considered is the skier's second — not the first, even if it were better.

Great care and consideration is given to the planning of a course. The principal factor is increased width upon the course commensurate with greater speeds as the racer descends the mountain. Forerunners, usually two or three, go down the mountain course before the racers to test the terrain and prepare the piste.

Men's courses usually have a drop of between 850m–1,000m. Women's courses are slightly less steep, between 400 and 700m. In events such as the world championships and Olympic Games, men's races must take more than two minutes from top to bottom; women's must run for not less than one minute and forty seconds.

Three days of training before a race itself are normal. Competitors seldom push themselves to the limit in these runs, preferring to keep something back for the race itself and give few clues to rivals as to their current form. But a run without stops on the final day of training is mandatory, whatever the eventual time.

GIANT SLALOM COURSE

GIANT SLALOM FLAGS

Open gate

Open gate

50cm

1m

75m

30cm

Closed or blind gate

SINGLE-POLE SLALOM

PARALLEL SLALOM

9

Rules/2

Slalom

The term slalom is of Norwegian origin and the first competitive slaloms were decided on style rather than time. It was Sir Arnold Lunn who in 1922 devised the first modern slalom run at Mürren. This introduced the racing element, with time the key factor.

In slalom, two runs comprise a single race, each run on a differently designed course. The two times are added together and the fastest skier in total is the winner. Slalom racing makes different demands on skiers; strong thighs, as in downhill, are a necessity but technique and control are of much greater importance.

The course is full of tightly placed gates (two poles) and requires turning technique, speed on short runs, balance, deft manoeuvring and strength. It places great demands on the skier, who is racing against the clock on a course full of dangers if he or she presses too hard in attempting to save time.

Flags on the gate poles are blue and red with each gate between 4 and 5m wide. The course must contain open and vertical gates and two or three vertical combinations (including between three and five gates) and at least four hair-pin combinations where the distance between the two verticals must be 0.85m.

Gates are numerous: on the men's courses, between fifty-five and seventy-five; on the women's courses, between forty and sixty. Gates are not allowed to be set so as to become too difficult for manoeuvring but they must test the skier's control under pressure of the clock. Failure to pass through all the gates designated, with both skis on the correct side, means disqualification. Fluency is the key to slalom racing. It is required through tight, closed gates and even past open gates and on the long, clear run-in to the finishing line.

At the end of the first run, the leading five skiers are reversed, ie the fastest on the first run goes last of the top five on the second run, giving him the slight advantage of knowing what time he has to achieve. But, as with downhill racing, it is not unknown for a slalom skier to come from the pack and, from a position hitherto assumed impossible, to clinch the race with an extremely fast second run.

Giant slalom

Giant slalom is a race of greater distance than ordinary slalom and there are other differences. Competitors can select their own line through the gates from faster sections or turning points, as in downhill racing. Races are held on hills providing some unusual twists and turns, although dangerous hills are not considered. In fact, giant slalom is a discipline between downhill and slalom racing. It is faster than slalom yet retains the importance of gates.

Gates are extended in width to compensate for the increase in speed — they are 4–8m wide and there are from fifty to seventy of them. Giant slalom demands from the skier the instant selection of the fastest and most direct route down the one mile course. Good edging — that is the control of the edge of the ski to stop sliding too wide around gates — is the essence of the discipline.

Cross-country

Cross country *(langlauf)* is most popular in the Scandinavian countries and these races are included in the Olympic Games. Distances vary from 10km to 50km. Very light skis are worn in this discipline with only the toe-end fixed permanently to the ski. Many hundreds of these races are held all over Scandinavia during the winter months, providing a test of technique, strength, fitness and consistency. It is a marathon on skis.

Forty years on:
Sir Arnold Lunn at
Mürren
where he devised
the first modern
slalom course in 1922.

11

Rules/3

Ski jumping

Ski jumping is the last of the major disciplines. One factor is required above all others in this most demanding of sports — courage, and plenty of it. To launch oneself from the top of a ramp overlooking a thin airstrip of snow well below, with a town laid out before the skier, is a daunting affair.

As regards the jump, distance is by no means the only criterion. Neatness is important because marks are awarded for style, both in the air and in the landing. So the jumper who flies longest through the air could find himself reaching the most distant landing point without leading the field at the end of the round.

It is a sport of grace and beauty as befits men who fly through the air like eagles. The sloping channel is termed the run-in and upon reaching the end of the ramp, the jumper must attempt to lean forward, hands and arms rigidly down each side of his body, in as motionless a position as possible. The skis should be close together and parallel until just before landing when one is eased in front of the other and the knees bent to absorb the impact of landing.

Timing and style are all important, more so than brute strength — although the ability to 'explode' off the launching ramp and attain a soaring effect throughout the flight is particularly important, in staying in the air longest and therefore achieving greatest distance. Ski jump ramps are normally 90m or 70m — although smaller runs are used.

In major competitions there are five judges, with the highest and lowest scores discarded to eliminate any suggestion of bias. Each judge can award a maximum of twenty points per jump with a fall costing the jumper ten points.

Two jumps must be made, with the marks for distance and style added together. The ski jumper with the highest total wins the event. In major competitions, falls are comparatively rare but jumpers lose marks for poor style during the flight or on landing. Both areas are scrutinised by the judges. Waving the arms in the air, allowing skis to cross and generally untidy jumping cost the competitor points.

Unlike other ski disciplines, aids such as ski-poles are not permitted on the ramp. Jumpers immediately adopt a crouching position on the ramp to achieve maximum speed on take-off. Judges allow competitors to use their arms for balance on landing; a necessary aid in steadying the human frame as it drops onto the hard snow below the jumping ramp.

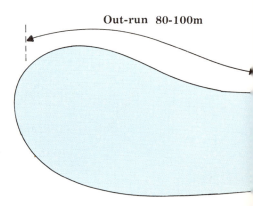

Out-run 80-100m

A jumper in action during the 1982 world
championships.

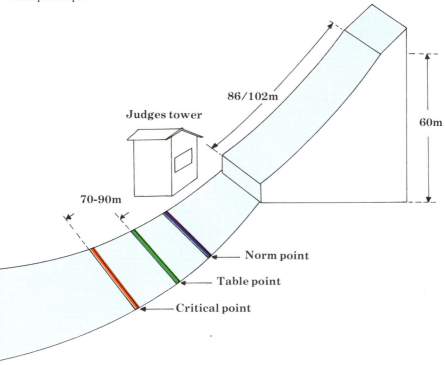

86/102 m

Judges tower

60m

70-90m

Norm point

Table point

Critical point

Rules/4

The leading ski jumpers come from Austria, Scandinavia, East Germany and North America. Austrian jumpers like Schnabl, Innauer, Neuper and Kogler have all left their mark upon the sport.

Youngsters in the mountain villages start learning to jump at tender ages. The forerunner sent down to help prepare the course in major events is often as young as thirteen — too young to compete, but practised in task which carries obvious dangers.

A major mistake in mid-air or on take-off from the launching pad could result in serious injury, paralysis or death. That much is clear to all the jumpers and outside influences can play a key role. A sudden gust of wind, blowing in an unexpected direction, can tip the skis dangerously or force the jumper to lose balance.

In Europe, the Four Hills event, held traditionally each New Year, is the most prestigious of the competitions, outside the Olympic Games. The four hills are in West Germany and Austria — at Oberstdorf, Garmisch-Partenkirchen, Innsbruck and Bischofschofen — and the competition is spread over a few days with the first day's jumping normally just before New Year's Eve. World championships and World Cup competitions are also held, with the latter decided by points awarded throughout the season on individual competitions.

Scandinavia boasts the Norwegian town of Holmenkollen as the home of ski jumping. Interest throughout Norway is extraordinary when the World cup circus is in town, often attracting crowds of 100,000.

Ski jumping's first official tournament was held in Norway, in Oslo in 1879, the groundwork prepared for such an event by the Norwegian who invented a method of retaining control of skis through proper binding while in the air — Sondre Norheim. From

Right, Holmenkollen's flying circus: the panoramic scene at the 1982 ski jumping world championships in Norway; and the anatomy of a jumping ramp.

Norheim's simple idea, a popular sport has taken wing.

The quality and strength of Scandinavian jumpers was underlined by the merit table list of top ten jumpers in the 1982–3 winter programme. The world champion was the Finn, Nydaenen. But other Finns highly ranked in the world include Nokkonen and Puikkonen, with Norwegians such as Hansson, Bergerud, Braaten and Bremseth also well respected.

14

Canada provided the runner-up in the 1982–3 series — Bulau. Another Canadian, Steve Collins, made a startling impact some seasons back when he first appeared on the world stage. Collins, of part Indian parentage, confirmed the belief that Red Indians have no fear of heights by leaping an astonishing 114.5m in the 1980 Olympics at Lake Placid. He was the youngest competitor in the event when he made his first appearance before the world's cameras at the age of fifteen, yet he seemed perfectly at ease on the death defying hill.

The gold medallist at Lake Placid on the 90m jump was yet another Finn, Tormanen. He just beat the Austrian, Neuper, who jumped 90m for the first time at fourteen years of age and had

handsome compensation by winning the 1980 and 1981 Four Hills event in West Germany and Austria.

Stams, a famous university near Innsbruck is recognised as the breeding and training ground for ski jumping. Here, jumpers such as Neuper and Kogler, the latter 1981 overall World cup champion, learn their trade from experts.

Undeterred by their lack of alpine hills on which to practise, the East Germans have created several plastic 'mountains' to compete with the best. Training can be carried on with that ruthless, disciplined approach common to Iron Curtain countries and the East Germans are always tough opponents to beat, whatever their natural disadvantages.

The Stars

Franz Klammer

Franz Klammer forged his reputation as the world's most exciting downhill ski racer on the strength of one extraordinary race lasting little more than one hundred seconds. On such fleeting moments of inspiration are built the success stories of a lifetime!

Klammer, who had first appeared on the downhill circuit in 1973, won the race of his lifetime to foil his Swiss rival, Bernard Russi, in the Olympic Games downhill race at Innsbruck in 1976. No one who saw the run made by Klammer is ever likely to forget it, such was its magnetic appeal for bravery, dash, verve and skill.

Russi, the pre-race favourite, was the man to beat in most experts' opinion. When the fine Swiss skier raced down the mountain in a time of 1 min 46.6 sec, no one, not even Klammer, seemed to have the remotest chance of denying Russi the gold medal. The time was far superior to any other that day — except Klammer's. Immortal actions, immortal words are carved upon the memory and, as Klammer was about to set off, the words of his coach are testimony to the courage required in this thrilling yet dangerous sport.

After Russi had stunned the Austrian crowd, Klammer asked his coach at the top of the mountain what he had to do to win. The coach, omitting the exact time details which would have shaken men even of Klammer's calibre, replied: 'Throw yourself down the mountain and pray.'

Klammer, ski-poles whirling in the air like some self-propelled helicopter, attempted the impossible. To the disbelief of neutrals and acclaim of a nation, he broke the finishing line in a time of 1 min 45.73. He had come down the mountain at speeds well in excess of eighty miles an hour, lived — and earned himself a place in skiing history.

Klammer has been a World cup downhill winner all over Europe from Garmisch to Gröden, Val d'Isère to Wengen, Madonna to Morzine. Born on 3 December 1953 at Mooswald, he never became the great technical skier hitherto believed essential to win consistently on the mountains. But raw courage, a great determination to succeed and a disregard for personal safety took Franz Klammer to the highest peak in world skiing.

After his first downhill World cup success at Schladming in 1973, Klammer was a consistent winner — until a sudden barren spell around the start of the 1980s. No one could explain it, least of all Klammer. He said: 'It lasted for three years and I did not know what to do. I could not find the right line down the mountain and so I had no chance to beat anybody. I was down, I lost my whole confidence, yet I did not know why it had happened.

'Quite suddenly, I had lost my best form and could not find it again. It was as much a mystery to me as to other people. After three years without the crowds, I knew what it was like to lose — very different from when the people surrounded me after victories. Yes, I missed that.'

Quite suddenly, as quickly as he had lost it, Klammer felt his old form once more within his grasp. 'I was training in late 1981 and I began to make good times once more. Then I made the best time and I knew it had come back. Yet I still don't know why it came back or why it went away in the first place.'

Klammer dominated downhill racing at his prime. There were few, if any, peers. Yet he says: 'These days it is much more difficult for one man to excel. 'The top skiers are closer together and maybe any man from fifteen racers could win a race. It was not like that a few years back.'

The season 1982-3 was an extra-

Franz Klammer on his way to the gold
medal in the 1976 Olympic Games at
Innsbruck. Inset: Klammer is protected by
police from enthusiastic fans after his great
win.

ordinary one — for skiing and for Klammer. Bad weather disrupted so much of the programme that continuity and rhythm were impossible for most of the time. It meant that previous champions of the 1980s, like Weirather and Podborski, were unable to find the same consistency which had brought them their titles.

In a season which produced so many different winners — including comparative unknowns such as Pfaffenbichler, Höflehner, Brooker and Kernan — Klammer quietly, yet gradually found the form which had eluded him for so long. He alone among the top skiers managed continuity in performance and, at the age of 29, it was enough to give him the downhill championship for the fifth time.

The outcome of the championship was in doubt until the climax of the season's final race at Lake Louise in the Canadian Rockies. Several skiers could have won the title but the two who were to fight it out were Klammer and the Swiss star, Conradin Cathomen. Klammer finished two tenths of a second ahead of the Swiss skier and thereby clinched second place behind the race winner (Höflehner). So he secured a sufficient number of points to lift the downhill title once more.

It was an enormous tribute to the man's courage, perseverance and competitiveness, not to say his skiing ability. Yet even Klammer doubts whether *all* the old daredevil qualities are still there. He says: 'I am not the same skier as years ago. Skiing is still a big thing for me, but life is a big thing too, nowadays.'

Franz Klammer, who has experienced a recent revival after a barren spell at the beginning of the 1980s.

The Stars/3

Phil Mahre

Phil Mahre stands the theory that practice makes perfect in all sports right on its head. The brilliant American slalom specialist has talents in other disciplines such as giant slalom and downhill and this has made him arguably the greatest all round skier of our times. But he is no devotee of the time-honoured method of becoming a world champion.

Phil is the younger brother of Steve Mahre by about four minutes — they were born on 10 May 1957. He is a natural skier, unlike the textbook-trained creatures pervading the modern sporting scene. It is fortunate, says Mahre, that he was American and not shackled by a national skiing squad such as the Swiss or the Austrian. Otherwise, he might never have emerged, because of his refusal to adhere to rigid restrictions in his life in pursuit of skiing excellence.

Mahre says: 'I like skiing and it's a hell of a nice pastime. But I ski for enjoyment, pure and simple. If I win races, that is fine; if I lose, it is nothing too serious. I am a competitive person by nature but I don't believe in long training sessions. Nothing is worth all that hassle because my belief is, if you do not feel like training one particular day, you should not have to do it.'

Such views are, of course, a direct contradiction of everything which the Austrian and Swiss ski experts believe. So Mahre is right in thinking that he would never have broken through to the top had he been from those countries.

Mahre's ability to stay at the top — to have got there in the first place — indicates a rich natural talent nurtured by only occasional training. Mahre is very much his own man and does his own thing, most of the time. If that includes winning races, that is fine. If it means disappointments, so be it. The big American would never sit down for hours analysing defeats.

His great challenge on the legendary Swede, Ingemar Stenmark, has made him one of the top men on the slalom slopes. But Mahre is much more than a slalom expert, as results have proved such as his fifth place in the downhill race at St Anton in 1983. It is by competing in the downhill that Mahre earns points in other disciplines away from slalom. Stenmark refuses to do that on a regular basis and so Mahre picks up points which help him to become the overall champion for the combined disciplines.

He is a great respecter of Stenmark but says: 'I have never idolised people in anything, sport or anything else. Ingemar and I respect one another enormously but I am my own person. He has a phenomenal record but I never take too much notice of statistics.'

Mahre is at his happiest away from the bright lights and glitter of the European circuit, in the mountains near his North American home. There he can lead the kind of quiet, basic life he prefers — somewhat unusual for a man from one of sport's most prestigious, jet-setting circuits.

'At this time, I still enjoy skiing and would like to continue for a while,' he says. 'But I shall continue only in my own way, in the style I prefer, certainly not in the European style. Too much importance is placed upon winning at all costs. Personally, I like to compete and see the beauty of the mountains on my way down. There must be more to life than making your heart thump just for the turn of a clock's hands.'

Phil Mahre, the self-possessed Canadian who is a brilliant all-round skier. He skis for fun, refusing a rigid commitment to the sport, and this attitude would keep him out of the top European squads.

The Stars/4

Karl Schranz (Austria)

Schranz, born in 1938, came from St Anton and rapidly developed into one of Austria's greatest ski heroes. His career is full of success. He thought he had won the giant slalom gold medal in Grenoble.

His career spanned thirteen years during which time he won races all over Europe. He also won many World championships and an Olympic silver medal although his Olympic achievements were tarnished in 1972 when he was disqualified for professionalism.

Jean-Claude Killy (France)

He won immortal fame for his achievement in winning three gold medals at the 1968 Winter Olympics in Grenoble. Born in France in 1944 he spent much of his early life on skis in the famous ski resort of Val d'Isère.

Killy dominated the Olympics on his native snow and won the gold for downhill, slalom and giant slalom — a feat virtually impossible in modern skiing.

Killy was at the height of his powers as a 24-year-old at the Grenoble Olympics. Before that he had won the downhill and combined gold medals in the 1966 world championships at Portillo, Chile, to announce his extraordinary talent.

At Grenoble, Killy swept the floor but his success was by no means widely and popularly received. Such was the gulf between him and others that claims of 'professionalism' were voiced, causing one of the greatest controversies in the skiing world. He kept his medals and they were to prove the launching pad for brief careers in films, motor racing and professional skiing.

Jean-Claude Killy

22

Gerhard Pfaffenbichler (Austria)
Downhill

Born 26 March 1961 at Unken, he is one of the tallest men on the downhill circuit at 6ft 2in and inconvenienced by the fact. A former policeman, he entered the top ten of the world rankings at the start of the 1980s but slipped back for a while.

He showed his ability by coming from nowhere to win the 1983 downhill race at Sarajevo, Yugoslavia. He squeezed into the Austrian top squad that day because of the unavailability of others!

Because of his size, gliding is the weakest part of his racing technique, because it is difficult to find the low tuck so vital in reducing wind resistance. But he has good technique on the turns for such a big man and could become a consistent winner on the world downhill circuit.

The Stars/5

Vladimir Andreev (USSR) Slalom
Like his Russian colleagues on the downhill circuit, Tsyganov and Makeev, Andreev failed to make the expected progress on the world rankings list in 1983 after showing good form in 1980 and 1981. Born on 9 February 1958 in Noskh his best result was second place in the slalom at Kitzbühel in 1981. Also that season, he was third at Oslo and fourth at St Anton. He finished ninth in the 1980 Olympics at White Face, United States.

Michel Canac (France) Slalom
A comparative newcomer to the slalom circuit, Canac finished fourth in the final race of the 1983 European season, on the St Anton Kandahar, behind the Mahre twins and Wenzel. He was born on 2 August 1956 at Aime and seemed slow to graduate into the elite club of top class slalom experts. He started on the World cup circuit in 1981–2 and his best race that season was at Garmisch, where he came fourteenth.

Paeola de Chiesa (Italy) Slalom
The number one in the Italian camp in 1982–3, his tendency towards adventure on the tricky slalom slopes has been his undoing on more occasions than one. Born on 14 March 1956 at Sauze d'Oulz he has skied World cup slaloms since 1975 without fulfilling the promise shown in his first season when he finished tenth on aggregate. During the 1974–5 season, he finished second at Madonna, third at Wengen and Kitzbühel and fifth at Garmisch — startling achievements for a newcomer to the scene but subsequent results have been spoiled by his impetuousness.

Fall guy: Apjok, of Hungary, takes a tumble in a downhill race at Val d'Isere.

Peter Müller (Switzerland) Downhill

Strongest and most consistent racer on the downhill circuit for some seasons, he has been the Swiss number one for five years. Fiercely competitive, a magnificent glider (easily the best on the circuit), Müller has been troubled by injuries which have prevented him in the last two years taking honours considered well within his reach.

He won his first downhill race at Villars in 1979 and also finished first at Gröden that season. He has been a consistent winner or highly placed finisher ever since, although the Austrians have tended to have the better of him in recent seasons. He was fifth in the world championships of 1978 and fourth in the 1980 Olympics.

Born at Adliswil on 6 October 1957, he was World cup downhill champion in 1980 and has the ideal physique for the discipline. If he had a weakness earlier in his career, it may have been on the turns but he worked hard to improve that aspect. He might have won the 1981 world championship but fell in Wengen when well-placed in the overall standings.

He concentrates hard in every race but felt that 1983 was a disappointing season because he gained no victories. However, he remains one of the top skiers in the world.

Steve Mahre (USA) Slalom

Older brother (by just four minutes) of his twin, Phil, he was the outsider of the two, until the 1982 world championships at Schladming, when he won the gold medal ahead of Phil (who fell) and Stenmark. Born on 10 May 1957 at White Pass, he had been winning slalom races as early as 1978 when he came first at Mount Stratton. But he did not enjoy his brother's outstanding success. However, he closed the gap in 1983 when a special slalom victory at St. Anton was his best result. That victory took Steve to the top of the 1983 slalom points table, ahead of both Phil and Stenmark.

He finished eighth in the 1978 slalom at the world championships but was a disappointing fifteenth in the giant slalom at the 1980 Olympics at Lake Placid. Technically, he was not quite as strong as his brother in earlier years but has improved to close the gap between the two.

Toni Bürgler (Switzerland) Downhill

Born on 17 August 1957 at Richenbach, he has been a regular member of the Swiss premier squad in recent seasons. A daredevil downhill racer, lack of concentration has often resulted in spectacular spills, thus ruining his chances of turning potential into success.

He won at Crans Montana in 1979, a win which seemed likely to be the first of many. It has not happened quite that way since. He has suffered some serious crashes, notably in the 1980 St Anton race. But until the emergence of Conradin Cathomen in the 1982 season, he was regarded as the Swiss number two behind Peter Müller.

Werner Grissman (Austria)
Downhill

Now virtually retired after a career spanning nine years on the downhill circuit, he works as a skiing commentator and analyst for Austrian TV and retains his close links with the racers who were once his colleagues. Regarded as a great character on the circuit during his years of competition, his nickname, not surprisingly, was 'The Grizzly'.

Born in Lienz on 21 January 1952, he shot to fame by winning the 1973 downhill race at St Moritz in his first season on the circuit. But this did not herald many more successes, although he finished third in the 1978 world championships and seventh at the Lake Placid Olympics in 1980.

Peter Lüscher (Switzerland) Slalom/Downhill

He was considered a slalom man for many years although his fourth place at Aspen in the 1976 downhill race underlined his abilities in all disciplines. Perhaps his greatest win was in the 1983 race at St Anton where he shocked the ski world — and the best of the downhillers — by snatching victory from the likes of Read, Podborski, Müller, Weirather and Stock.

A fine all-round skier as his record suggests, he was born in Romanshorn on 14 October 1956. He won the slalom at Garmisch in 1979, the combination at Schladming a year earlier and combination at Garmisch and Gröden, also in 1979. He has had many second, third, fourth and fifth placings in all events but has never quite produced such form in world championship or Olympic races.

Silvano Meli (Switzerland) Downhill

Born in 1960, his second place in the 1983 downhill race at St Anton — the famous Arlberg-Kandahar — confirmed Swiss optimism as to his bright future. He was not in the top Swiss squad last season but good form throughout 1983 was confirmed by that triumph at St Anton.

He is the logical successor, eventually, to older Swiss men such as Müller but, ironically, he had some of his chances only because of injuries to team mates such as Müller, Heinzer and Bürgler. Bruno Kernan, another Swiss, also came through strongly in 1983, winning at Kitzbühel in the first race on the Hahnenkamm.

Toni Bürgler

28

Paul Frommelt (Liechtenstein) Slalom

He and Andreas Wenzel form a brilliant slalom combination from the tiny principality of Liechtenstein. That such a small country should produce superb skiers is not so surprising because it has close associations with the sport.

In fact, skiing is by far the most popular sport in Liechtenstein which is dominated by areas such as Malbu and Triesenberg. Wenzel's sister, Hanni, is another fine exponent of slalom skiing and she won the gold medal in both the slalom and giant slalom in the 1980 Olympics at Lake Placid.

Frommelt was born on 9 August 1957 at Schaan and has been winning slalom races since 1979 when he triumphed at Crans Montana. But inevitably his outright successes have been reduced by the presence of the extraordinary Swede, Stenmark, who has dominated slalom for almost eight years.

His best all-round season was in 1977, when he finished runner-up at Laax and Wengen, third at St. Anton, fourth at Sun Valley and Are, fifth in Berchtesgaden, sixth at Kitzbühel and seventh at Furano. A splendid example of consistent racing.

Ingemar Stenmark (Sweden) Slalom

Stenmark lays claim, and rightly so, to the tag of 'the world's greatest ever slalom skier'. He has an astonishing record since he first appeared on the slalom circuit back in 1974. From 1976 to 1981, he had few genuine challengers. His sequence of wins is overwhelming and he has recorded victories all over the world in every race of importance.

He finished first in the slalom and giant slalom at both the 1978 World Championships and the 1980 Olympics. A coveted double in each case which, if any doubt ever existed, confirmed him as undisputed number one in the world.

Born on 18 March 1956, he learned his skiing near his home of Tärnaby in the mountains of northern Sweden and won his first European circuit race at Madonna, Italy, in 1974. Successes in both slalom and giant slalom followed with almost boring repetition and only the emergence of Phil Mahre provided some kind of serious challenge.

A withdrawn, shy man, he prefers to let his record do the talking. His toughest opponent, Phil Mahre, pays him a rich tribute, saying: "Ingemar

has proved he is the best technical skier ever to come to the sport. His record is phenomenal."

Stenmark earned a reputation as a man capable of a remarkable second run which took him to countless titles. 'The Stenmark charge' it became known as and, time and time again, destroyed opponents who felt a rare success over the master was within sight.

Bojan Krizaj (Yugoslavia) Slalom

Yugoslavia's number one slalom racer, he has trailed in Stenmark's wake — like so many others — since he first arrived on the scene in 1977. He won the slalom at Wengen in 1980 and finished second at Madonna (1979) and Chamonix (1980). He also finished runner-up in the giant slalom at Jasna, Val d'Isère and Heavenly Valley all in 1979.

Krizaj was fourth in the 1980 Olympic giant slalom but, despite great ability, still struggles to get past the combined talents of Stenmark and the Mahre twins, Steve and Phil. He was born on 3 January 1957 in Kranj and on his day is one of the best competitors in slalom racing. The weakness of his racing is that he often pushes himself too hard and skis out, thus missing a gate and being disqualified.

A rare defeat for Ingemar Stenmark, Sweden's slalom king (left). His conqueror on this occasion was the Yugoslavia, Krizaj, in a race in 1980 at Wengen, with Liechtenstein's Paul Frommelt (right) in third place.

Vladimir Makeev (USSR) Downhill

He has yet to match the achievement of Tsyganov, who became the first Soviet downhiller to win a race on the world circuit. Both men have been surprisingly slow to close the gap between the best of the Europeans and the Soviets, which is apparent even today.

Born on 10 September 1957 in Kemenovo, he finished third in the downhill at Schladming in 1978, but has enjoyed few highlights since then. He finished a disastrous twenty-second in the 1980 Olympic downhill.

Leonhard Stock (Austria) Downhill

Born on 14 March 1958, Stock unexpectedly won the Olympic gold in the 1980 downhill race on White Face mountain. Stock is unhappy on tight, twisting course which includes jumps, but he was entirely at home at Lake Placid in conditions which might have been specially created for him. He was the sensation of the training runs and duly won the gold, thus raising the question of importance of the Olympics, for he had done little of note during the European season.

Since then, Stock has not approached the top three racers in the world with any consistency. He has never won a downhill race in the World cup although he finished second at Villars in 1979, behind Müller.

Steve Podborski (Canada) Downhill

The 1982 world champion, Podborski changed his style and took more care for his personal safety. This brought him consistency and the world title. In beating Weirather to the title he displayed all the required qualities — skill, consistency, perseverance and courage. The latter, in fact, was often his undoing because he pressed too hard on the most difficult mountains.

He had a disappointing season in 1983, but still beat all-comers on his best form. Podborski won his first downhill race at Morzine in 1979 and steadily improved after that, as the Canadians became more professional in their approach. But when he became champion, it was an immense achievement for the comparatively small and financially embarrassed Canadian squad, which had few of the luxuries enjoyed by the Austrians.

Podborski was born on 25 July 1957 in Don Mills and lives in Ontario. He worked hard to sharpen up on the turns and jumps. An ideal size and weight for a downhiller, his squat frame clad in the Canadians' yellow catsuits has become a familiar sight on the European circuit. In 1982 he repaid the faith of the International Skiing Federation who, somewhat surprisingly, gave him number one rating ahead of the 1981 downhill champion Harti Weirather, his friend and close rival.

Stig Strand (Sweden) Slalom

Strand comes from Tärnaby, the same town in northern Sweden as his close friend, Stenmark. He has been saddled with the onerous title of being tipped as Stenmark's successor by some commentators, although he is the same age — born on 25 August 1956.

He has been on the World cup slalom circuit since 1976 but before the 1982–3 season he did not catch the eye consistently. He was fifth at Madonna in 1980 but results in 1983 suggested better days were just around the corner.

Peter Wirnsberger (Austria) Downhill

Wirnsberger is one of the younger members of the Austrian squad and a skier with a promising future, judging by results in the early part of his career. Born in 1958, he made a startling entry into the downhill scene by winning three races in the 1979 calendar — at Garmisch, Lake Placid and Val d'Isère. He had a second place at Kitzbühel that year, too. Despite other successes — notably the silver medal in the 1980 Olympics behind Leonhard Stock — the following two seasons were major disappointments for him and for the Austrians.

Valeri Tsyganov (USSR) Downhill

Accident-prone on several occasions since his first appearance in 1979, he established a place in skiing history by winning the 1981–2 downhill at Aspen, Colorado, to become the first Soviet skier to win a World cup race.

Born on 4 February 1961, he is still young enough to develop into the major threat expected of the Soviet number one downhiller. So far, that threat has not materialised. He finished eighth in the 1980 Olympic downhill.

Steve Podborski

Konrad Bartelski (UK) Downhill

Bartelski, senior member of the British ski team, is now nearing the end of his career. But he has been an inspiration to British skiers. Never has the country sent so many young skiers to European competitions or shown such enthusiasm for top racers, prompted by television coverage and Bartelski's success in the 1981–2 season. 'If I can do it, then so can others' is Bartelski's motto.

He has skied for Britain in three Olympic Games, finishing twelfth in the Lake Placid downhill in 1980. His best finishing place in a World cup race was a second in the 1981–2 downhill at Val Gardena, only hundredths, of a second behind the winner, Erwin Resch, of Austria. Despite a heavy cold on that day, Bartelski amazed the crowd, the British team and himself with a fine run.

He started the 1982–3 season in the ranks of the top fifteen downhill skiers in the world, for the first time. However, his performance that season was disappointing. He was sixteenth in 1982 world championships at Schladming.

Bartelski was born in Amsterdam on 27 May 1954 — his mother is British, his father Polish. He is based in London but spent several years in Austria. Although he is by far the most experienced member of the British squad, there are several youngsters showing signs of following in his footsteps. One of the up and coming Britons is Martin Bell, a seventeen year old from Edinburgh who attends a ski school in Stams, near Innsbruck.

The Stars/12

Ken Read (Canada) Downhill

Until the emergence of Todd Brooker in the 1983 Hahnenkamm race at Kitzbühel, Read and Podborski carried the entire Canadian team. The older members, Dave Irwin and Dave Murray, were not in the class of Read or Podborski, once known as the 'Kamikaze Canadians'.

Read was born on 6 November 1955 in Calgary and made a sensational start on the downhill circuit, winning the 1975 Val d'Isère race in his first season. After that, he had to wait three years for his next win at Chamonix. Schladming was another victory in 1978.

Gradually, Read forged a reputation as Canada's leading light until Podborski emerged. But Read disappointed everyone, including himself, by falling in the 1980 Olympics where he was fancied to win the gold medal. Friendly, genuine and dedicated, Read is now approaching the climax to his career. He may find outright successes harder to come by as younger men such as Brooker take over.

Andreas Wenzel (Liechtenstein)
Slalom/Downhill

Wenzel takes part in all three disciplines — slalom, giant slalom and downhill — although the first of these is his greatest strength. He won the combination title at the Garmish world championships of 1978 and earned the silver medal at the 1980 Olympics in the giant slalom.

He has been on the World cup circuit since 1977 and his downhill results are still improving, as positions in the top nine of races near the end of the 1982–3 season illustrated. He won two giant slaloms in 1978, his first year of serious competition, and has been in the top five almost ever since on the slalom slopes. He finished fourth in the downhill race on Kitzbühel's feared Hahnenkamm mountain, in 1980 — a great achievement for a skier considered a slalom specialist. Born on 18 March 1958 at Planken, his slalom victories have been limited by the extraordinary prowess of Stenmark.

The Stars/13

Todd Brooker (Canada) Downhill

He announced his arrival when he finished second in a 1981–2 World cup race at Aspen, Colorado, and went one better in the Aspen race of the 1982–3 season. He had a chance of the overall men's downhill title after winning the coveted Kitzbühel Hahnenkamm race earlier in the season. In the final race at Lake Louise, Canada, Brooker looked set to win but fell within sight of the finish. As a result, he finished a close-up ninth in the overall downhill standing.

Born on 24 November 1959 at Waterloo, Ontario, Brooker is in the mould of the 'Kamikaze' Canadians, especially the fearless Podborski, upon whom he modelled himself. Good results in season 1981–2 — such as fifth on Vancouver's perilous Whistler Mountain, ninth in the first Aspen race and second in the other Aspen event — earned him a seeded starting position in the 1982–3 season and his displays fully justified that.

Doris de Agostini (Switzerland) Downhill

The tall, elegant figure of Doris de Agostini has been unmistakeable on the downhill slopes in the past two seasons. Although her first World cup downhill win was in 1976 at Gastein, followed by two wins at Schruns and Megève and second place at Pfronten, Megève and Crans in 1981, she had few successes until the 1982–3 season when she devastated all opposition to clinch the World Cup downhill title.

Unlike many of the other women skiers, de Agostini concentrates all her efforts on the downhill. She came seventh in the Schladming world championships of 1982. She was born 28 April 1958 at Airolo.

Irene Epple (West Germany) Downhill/slalom/giant slalom

Irene Epple was born on 18 June 1957 in Seeg-Allgäu and since 1980 has been a consistent winner, especially in her favourite disciplines, downhill and giant slalom. Her first wins were in the giant slalom in 1980 at Saalbach and Val d'Isère but as far back as 1975 she gained a second place in the downhill at Val d'Isère.

Slalom is her weakest discipline which she constantly seeks to improve. She was silver medallist in the 1980 Olympics in the giant slalom and eighth in the downhill of the world championships in 1982.

Her younger sister, Maria, is rapidly nearing her sister's class and finished second to her in the 1982 World cup giant slalom. Maria was born on 11 March 1959, also in Seeg-Allgäu and her first World cup win was in the giant slalom at Zweisel in 1981.

Irene Epple

Tamara McKinney (USA) Slalom and giant slalom

Tamara McKinney has been one of the best of the rapidly improving American and Canadian contingent over the past couple of seasons. Born on 16 October 1962 at Olympic Valley in California, her first wins were recorded in the giant slalom in 1981 at Haute Nendaz, Les Gets and Aspen.

A fierce competitor, she came 6th in the overall World cup season of 1981 and rose to top place by the end of the 1983 season, ahead of such brilliant skiers Hanni Wenzel and Erika Hess. A skier to watch for the future.

Hanni Wenzel (Liechtenstein) Downhill/slalom/giant slalom

Born on 14 December 1956 in Planken, Hanni Wenzel is now nearing the end of a highly successful career. An excellent, all-round skier, Hanni had her first success in 1973 in the World Cup giant slalom at Zell-am-See. She has been a consistent performer ever since and did exceptionally well in the Olympics in 1980, where she gained second place in the downhill and won gold medals in both the slalom events.

Her brother Andreas, two years her junior, and younger sister Petra (born 20 November 1961) have also had outstanding successes on the circuit, with Petra improving all the time and finishing ninth in the World cup slalom at the end of the 1982–3 season.

Petra Wenzel

Erica Hess (Switzerland) Slalom and giant slalom

Erica Hess emerged as the finest all-round skier of the women's world championships at Schladming in 1982, taking first place in the slalom, giant slalom and combination event to scoop three gold medals. She was over-all World cup champion in 1982 and slalom champion from 1981–3.

She has fluency and great consistency and started her run of success in 1981 with six slalom wins (at Schruns, Crans Montana, Les Diablerets, Zweisel, Wangs and Furano) and one giant slalom win (Wangs). She also gained third place in the slalom at the 1980 Olympics.

Born on 6 March 1962 at Grafenort where she spent her childhood on her parents' small farm with five brothers and sisters, she began racing at five years old and was a surprising runner-up in the national championships at fourteen. At fifteen she left school to take up racing full time and quickly proved herself a calm, consistent skier with fantastic discipline. Her balance and quick reactions have been major ingredients of her success but she affirms: 'My style is my own.'

Cindy Nelson (USA) Downhill & Giant Slalom

Cindy Nelson is one of the top US women skiers and has been consistently successful over the past eleven seasons. She was born at Lutsen in Minnesota on 19 August 1956 and had her first World cup wins in 1974 in the downhills at Grindelwald and Saalbach. Her best disciplines are the downhill and giant slalom but her slalom is good enough to make her one of the best all-round skiers on the circuit.

She was seventh in the 1980 Olympics downhill and helped the US women's team to their first Nations cup victory in 1982. In the 1982 world championships she was second in the downhill and fourth in the combination, much to her disgust. (The top downhillers, men and women, feel the combination races give an unfair advantage to the slalom specialists with the downhillers penalised).

Cindy Nelson

43

Road to the top

Skiing's road to the top is a long, arduous climb demanding a variety of sacrifices, skills and slices of good fortune. So many parts combine to create a top class downhill racer or slalom specialist — and a small piece of luck can mean the difference between victory and second place.

The great names of skiing, such as Killy, Stenmark, Weirather and Klammer, took their first slippery sorties on skis as toddlers. As soon as youngsters can walk or get around, however uncertainly, they learn to ski if they come from the mountain villages where snow falls regularly every winter. This early start is imperative for future champions. Youngsters are natural on skis — they have no fear of skiing or snow.

As they grow up, they regard skiing as a normal activity, just as practical and natural as walking. Competitions start for skiers from the age of eight, when they start collecting cups and trophies.

To master the world's toughest mountain courses — such as Kitzbühel's Hahnenkamm and Wengen's Lauberhorn — requires more than sheer ability. Physique is a vital factor: strong thighs, wiry bodies and muscular arms to negotiate the punishing courses are equally important attributes.

The ideal weight for top-line racers on the downhill circuit is 75–80kg although agility is also vital. A greater weight would make turning a problem and this would be a big disadvantage. Talent means little without rigorous training to ensure that the body is in peak condition and techniques are perfected.

The European racing season for the downhillers might seem comparatively short — from late November or early December to the beginning of February, when the circuit crosses the Atlantic to Canada and the United States to decide the eventual overall World Cup winners. But after the North American races have ended, the skier's life is by no means quiet until the following winter in Europe.

During the summer months in the northern hemisphere, they travel long distances to train, as far away as South America (usually in the mountains of Chile) or to the slopes of New Zealand's Southern Alps. In those two settings, training can last for at least a month after the snow has disappeared from the European resorts.

The programme defies any suggestion that such a lengthy trip might be pleasurable. The former world champion, Harti Weirather, explains: You are there to train, to start your build-up for the following season, to keep your mind very much on skiing. Often, the individual would feel it might be nicer to be at home in Europe enjoying the sun and spending time on his hobbies. But there is not much time to think of those things in training camp.

'We normally train for four hours in the morning, then have lunch and do a further two hours work in the afternoon. That will include physical exercises as well as training runs down the mountains. In training camps in Europe just before the winter season begins around September or October, we train only Monday to Friday, whereas in summer training camp in New Zealand or Chile, we would work every day of the week including Sunday. It is a hard programme.'

Even when the skier does find some time to follow his own pursuits, it is often with an eye on his number one sporting activity. Many downhill skiers compete in motor cross events, riding bikes which help strengthen their leg muscles, particularly knees and thighs. Others, like Weirather, spend time in the mountains even when the snow has gone, running

Harti Weirather (Austria) Downhill

Weirather clinched the World cup downhill title in 1981 after a splendid season which included victories at St Anton and Aspen. He comes from the little village of Wängle near the Austrian/West German border and has been skiing — and winning competitions — since he was eight years old.

He thrilled Austria by winning the world championship gold medal at Schladming in 1982 to follow his World cup downhill victory the previous year. Stocky and compact, Weirather is probably the best technical downhill skier and his rise to the top has been rapid. He first appeared in 1979 and quickly impressed. Skilful at negotiating the tricky bends on difficult downhill courses, his compact body keeps him low to the ground in an effective tuck position.

He had a horrific crash as a sixteen-year-old in the Austrian national championships, falling 60m on his neck. He badly sprained neck muscles and still suffers pain from the injury. He also damaged a shoulder in that crash and continues to feel this old injury. Yet none of these injuries have affected him in a mental or physical sense. He remains a classic downhiller and ranks with the legendary Klammer among Austria's best.

Road to the top/2

down the slopes amid the thickest of the forests. The idea is to help the skier get used to selecting instantly the best line down a mountain. Training the eye and mind to make split-second decisions is a vital part of racing.

Weirather is known in the little Austrian village of Wängle, which is still his home, for a remarkable feat as a young boy. Skiing through the forest on part of a mountain, he swung around a turn and saw, straight in front of him, workmen repairing the track with a vehicle blocking his path. Even at that early age, he was able to make the snap decision required to avoid the obstacle — swerving onto a small hill which enabled him to jump the danger and land further down the mountain. Perfect preparation for a future world champion!

In all, the skiers train for seven months of the year, in addition to the three and a half months they spend in competition. The sport makes great demands upon the time of its top competitors. General technique would have been mastered by a racer before earning selection for the national squad.

Each country chooses four skiers for its premier squad and four for its second choice squad. Competition, especially in squads such as the Austrian and Swiss, is ferociously hot, with many good skiers often disappointed. Before the 1980 Olympic race, the Austrians were so unsure of their best line-up that a special training run was arranged. The four fastest men were to gain selection for the top squad, announced the coaches. The idea was bitterly criticised by the racers — but to no avail. Leonhard Stock, who was not expected even to earn a place in the top squad, won the time trial and went on to win the Olympic gold medal. This underlines the great depth of talent within the Austrian camp.

At the summit: Erica Hess has every reason to be delighted after winning the overall World cup in 1982.

Technique

Understanding the value of the low tuck position, that is when the skis are flat on the snow and the body is crouched very low to minimise wind resistance, is imperative. But the tuck position is especially tiring on the legs and back and great strength is required to maintain a long tuck.

As mentioned in the section on equipment in this book, waxing is important, although the development of special skis adapted to suit a variety of conditions is gradually minimising the value of this. But allowing the skis to remain flat on the icy piste for as much as possible of the run down the mountain is the secret of a fast time.

Being able to glide comes only with practice and experience. Men like the big Swiss skier, Peter Müller, are especially good at this — allowing the skis to stay flat and maintaining maximum speed at all times. The longer the downhiller spends in the air, the worse the time will be at the end of the run.

Peter Müller

47

Events

The events on the men's European winter circuit are the highlight of the season. Few sports can compete as a spectacle with the sight of zigzagging slalom stars and daredevil racers pouring down the crisp, icy snow of the mountains of Europe. It is dangerous, exhilarating, and full of atmosphere.

Every four years, the winter Olympic Games are held and the world championships also have a four-year cycle. These two major events are staggered so that there is always a two-year gap between them. The 1980 winter games were held on America's White Face Mountain, followed by the 1982 world championships at Schladming, Austria, and the 1984 Olympics in Sarajevo, Yugoslavia.

In late November or early December the World cup starts and, apart from a break for the Christmas and New Year period, continues until early February. Then the skiers leave Europe, sometimes for Sweden and then for North America where races are held in the Rocky Mountains at Aspen, Colorado, and over the border in the Canadian Rockies, sometimes at beautiful Lake Louise. Although North America can boast such thrilling settings as Vancouver's Whistler Mountain (often considered *too* dangerous), Europe — and particularly certain races — lays claim to be the summit of the season.

Thrills and spills are guaranteed; some races, like the Hahnenkamm above the little Austrian Tyrol town of Kitzbühel, are positively electrifying. If Kitzbühel's Hahnenkamm is arguably Europe's greatest race, not far behind comes the Lauberhorn event at Wengen, which is tucked away in the mountains between the Swiss city of Berne and the Simplon railway tunnel on the Italian border.

To reach the mountain which stages the Lauberhorn race, only two modes of transport are available — mountain railway or helicopter. Wengen, with its terrifying jumps and difficult twisting bends, is certainly one of the two toughest mountain courses in Europe. No wonder that for the downhill racers, a Kitzbühel-Wengen double is considered the ultimate achievement in the season — a Blue Riband of downhill racing. Both courses require supreme skill and, more especially, a liberal dose of bravery — merely to get down the mountain in one piece let alone in the fastest time of the day.

Races are held all over the mountains of Europe. Italy has centres such as Gröden, Madonna di Campiglio in the Dolomites, Val Gardena, Cortina, Aprica, Sansicario, Limone di Piemont, Piancavallo and Bormio which hold both men's and women's races, downhill and slalom, at various times of the year. Switzerland's sites include Crans-Montana, Haute Nendaz, Les Diablerets, St Moritz, Ebnat-Kappel, Adelboden, Grindelwald, Arosa and, of course, Wengen. In France, the centres are Val d'Isère — the traditional starting point for the first race of the European season — Les Gets, Megève, Morzine and Chamonix.

West German races are held at Garmisch-Partenkirchen, Bad Wiessee, Pfronten, Lenggries, Berchtesgaden, Zwiesel; with jumping at Oberstaufen. The Austrian venues include Kitzbühel, St Anton, Schruns, Altenmarkt, Haus, Schladming. In Yugoslavia, the 1984 Olympics will be held at Sarajevo on a specially created run full of jumps and unpredictable turns.

Points are awarded for each race in the World cup programme. The winner receives 25 points, the runner-up 20 and third 15. At the end of the season, the points are tallied and the skier with the highest number is the overall champion.

The Lauberhorn at Wengen (photograph supplied by the Swiss tourist office, London).

Kitzbühel

Kitzbühel is to skiing what Wimbledon is to tennis, Lord's to cricket, Twickenham to rugby. It is the natural home of ski racing, especially for downhill events. Few settings can match the marvellous atmosphere, the sight and sound of Kitzbühel on downhill day, which is always a Saturday.

In recent years, poor weather in other parts of Europe has meant postponed races being staged at Kitzbühel. This provides a double-header weekend with two downhills, on the Friday and Saturday, followed by slalom racing on Sunday. But a rearranged race on the same mountain with the same racers producing the same excitement does not attract the crowds.

But on the Saturday of a Kitzbühel weekend the scene is unequalled. From first light, thousands of visitors pour into the little town. Hemmed in by mountains on either side, Kitzbühel becomes besieged. Tourists come in summer and winter yet no influx bears comparison with this special invasion on the same Saturday each year.

The car parks stretch endlessly, full of Mercedes, BMWs, Porsches and Jaguars. Registration plates show visitors have travelled from all corners of Europe to be there: from Italy, Switzerland, West Germany (especially Munich), England and France (particularly Nice, Cannes and the other towns on the Côte d'Azur). The villages of Kitzbühel all turn out to watch the race and the influx of 'the beautiful people' — elegant and fashionable in their expensive ski suits, with time to spare and money to spend in the cafés, shops and restaurants.

The Hahnenkamm mountain dominates Kitzbühel. It towers above everything and some of the descents on its icy sides are terrifying even from a distance. Close up, they seem beyond the control of man but these top racers throw themselves without fear off such intimidating perches.

Two parts of the Hahnenkamm run are beyond compare for danger: the Mousefalle and the Stilehang. The Mousefalle is a sheer drop which requires a huge jump from the ledge above; the Stilehang is an icy, wickedly tight stretch with a perilous gradient and presents the racer with the severest test.

The weather, it seems, is so often good at Kitzbühel. Other races seem dogged by poor conditions or driving snow yet Kitzbühel appears charmed by brilliant sun and deep blue sky on the day of the big race each January. All morning, amateur skiers queue to take the chairlift to the top of the mountain, either to ski themselves or watch the racers start their runs. Of course, no one is allowed on the championship course, which is kept in pristine condition until the first of the forerunners descends.

The race begins in the middle of the day when conditions are at the best. It is still a slight disadvantage to go first when the course is at its iciest; it skis more quickly after a few runs have carved a track. At the top, the view down the mountain and across the range of surrounding peaks is stupendous. But controlling nerves and keeping concentration are the only things on the racer's mind, not the beauty of the view, splendid though it is.

It is possible for spectators to reach the top of the mountain and see the start without skis. But to watch on the side of the course from anywhere near halfway down the mountain, skis are required to take the enthusiast close to the action. For those who do not want to travel up the mountain — and queuing for the cable car can take a long time — the finish is a good position.

The first thrill is captured when a tiny, dark figure is glimpsed in the far distance. In reality, it is not at the very top of the mountain. But from the bottom, it is impossible to see the start of the race, which is so high up. On the first sighting the racer is more than two thirds of the way down and a skier pounding down the rest of the course creates a rumbling sound from the skis banging against the hard piste. It is a unique moment in winter sport and stirs the blood.

The crowd at the bottom will have grown to many thousands when the race starts. By the finish, it will be in a high state of excitement, especially if an Austrian is the winner. Local people take their skiing most seri-ously — it is, after all, the number one sport in Austria. The winner is feted, whatever his nationality. If he is an Austrian, however, he is more likely to be mobbed.

The first three men go off into the town for a press conference, followed by the presentation of cups and medals. For the packed press centre, it is a chance to meet the winners and question them on the race. For press and public the Hahkenkamm race at Kitzbühel is the biggest day of the downhill year. An experience not to be missed!

World Cup Scoring

Position	Points
1st	25
2nd	20
3rd	15
4th	12
5th	11
6th	10
7th	9
8th	8
9th	7
10th	6
11th	5
12th	4
13th	3
14th	2
15th	1

The Hahnenkamm at Kitzbühel (photo-graph supplied by the Austrian tourist office, London).

Equipment

In downhill, speed is the most important factor. Waxing applied to the bottom of the ski must be correct to suit the state of the piste. However brilliant and brave the skier, his or her efforts are likely to be undermined if the waxing applied to the skis is wrong. The importance to the skier of the national squads' back-up teams cannot be exaggerated.

Skis are normally made of fibreglass or plastic — materials which have generally replaced wood and metal. Edges of metal produce a tighter grip on the snow which is hardly the requirement of the downhill races. Skis can vary in weight and length depending upon individual preference. But for downhill racing they are heavier and harder than for the other events.

Sticks are an important part of the racer's equipment, to enable split second adjustment in balance and weight distribution. Yet the Austrian Erwin Resch won a bronze medal in the 1982 world championships at Schladming despite losing a ski-pole halfway down the mountain. This proved that ski-sticks are not indispensable.

The sticks are normally made of steel or aluminium tubing with plastic handles and an adjustable strap to fit the skier's hand. To aid speed, they are often bent halfway down the pole, so that they fit snugly round the racer's body. At the bottom of the stick is a smaller basket than on the slalom sticks, because the risk of falling into deep snow is not so great for the downhill men.

A racer's boots are strong, sturdy and designed to protect ankles and heels in the event of a fall. They are harder and higher-fitting than for cross-country skiing. Dress, too, is designed exclusively with speed in mind. Thick, cumbersome clothing would provide too much wind resis-

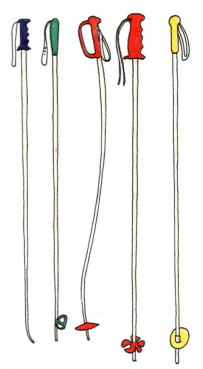

STICKS OR SKI-POLES

RACING BOOT

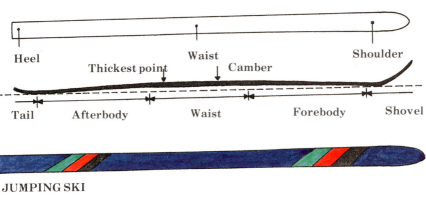

Heel · Waist · Shoulder
Thickest point · Camber
Tail · Afterbody · Waist · Forebody · Shovel

JUMPING SKI

DOWNHILL SKI

SLALOM SKI

tance and so modern racers wear tight-fitting, single-piece catsuits — almost like a second skin. Goggles are necessary to eliminate watery eyes and glare on the slope.

Crash helmets are mandatory for downhillers, who reach speeds approaching eighty miles an hour. Thick gloves are also worn. In slalom skiing, helmets are not required and knitted ski-hats are often worn. Most competitors wear goggles and much thicker, warmer suits than the downhillers.

Cross-country and jumping skis differ vastly from the downhill and slalom variety in that the bindings are only at the toe — rather than toe and heel — allowing the skier to 'run' on the snow. These skis are longer, thinner and lighter and are worn with much lighter footwear, almost like running shoes.

No special clothing is necessary for cross-country skiing. Although unwaxed skis can now be used and are suitable for beginners, serious competitors make sure the correct wax is applied to their waxable skis to suit conditions on the piste.

There are three main types of wax for different snow conditions and temperatures — hard, klister and glide. All are colour-coded — usually ranging from a green wax for fresh snow (below zero) to red klister for old, wet snow (40°F and above). Although some of the waxless skis are good, particularly the fishscale type, they cannot match a ski which is waxed for the prevailing conditions.

Cross-country ski-poles are longer and bend more easily than downhill/slalom sticks. They have a curved metal tip at the bottom, a rounded hand-grip and adjustable wrist-straps. They should be long enough to fit under the armpits. The baskets at the bottom of the poles should be wide enough to prevent the pole sinking into thick snow.

There is such a huge range of ski equipment available these days that beginners are advised to visit a specialist shop where experienced assistants can help choose the correct gear for particular activities.

Costs

The prices range enormously depending on whether the equipment is for the occasional two-week winter holiday enthusiast or for racing. The figures below contrast the costs for the holiday skier with those of the professional requiring the top standard equipment available.

	Ordinary	Top-class
Binding	£40	£90
Skis	£50	£250–£300
Suits	£80	£200–£250
Sticks	£8–£10	£30–£45
Gloves	£12	£40–£50
Goggles	£4–£5	£50–£60
Helmet	£15–£30	£100–£130
Hat	£5–£6	£25
Socks	£4	£15
Thermal underwear	£25	£55–£75
Boots	£40	£180–£240

Non-wax skis:

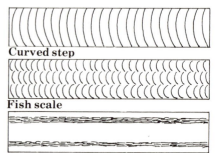

Curved step

Fish scale

Mohair strip

Binding: this differs with jumping and cross-country events having skis fastened only at the toe (rather than heel and toe as in other forms of racing).

Artificial snow

Man-made snow is now widely used in the United States and is gaining popularity in Europe. Alpine events are so much easier to arrange when snow is guaranteed and too much snow now tends to be more of a problem than too little.

Snow-making was pioneered in the United States ski resorts and the Lake Placid Olympics could not have been staged without it. Schladming, near Salzburg, Austria, has also installed snow guns, promoted perhaps by the poor and unreliable snowfalls of the past few winters.

Man-made snow is fine crystals created by atomised water being fired into the atmosphere by a type of gun in sub-zero temperatures. This snow can be made wet or dry depending on conditions, equipment and requirements. Because less air goes into each flake of artificial snow, 1in of man-made snow is worth 6in of natural snow.

Man-made snow also facilitates early training on mountains where natural snow does not fall till later in the season. Hundreds of thousands of tons of artificial snow can be manufactured to cover trails and slopes bereft of the real thing.

Goggles and crash helmet give Conrad Cathomen a space-age look, but they are essential to keep out the glare and for safety reasons. Note also the ski-poles which are bent to fit the contours of the racer's body.

Equipment/3

RACING KIT

Hats

Goggles

Bent poles

16

Gaiters

Boots

Skis

People in the media

Sports such as tennis, cricket, rugby and football are relatively straightforward for the purpose of television commentaries. The action is confined within a fairly small space, within the view of the man describing the scene for television viewers. However to produce words to match pictures from some of the steepest mountains in the world is by no means a simple exercise — as the very nature of the sport suggests.

The skiing commentator has to operate from a position which is almost totally devoid of atmosphere, yet capture the spirit and excitement of one of the world's most sensational sports. It is not an easy task. Commentators at big football matches, or beside Wimbledon's Centre Court, or at Lord's for a crucial Test match or at a packed Cardiff Arms Park rugby ground have the smell of action, the heat of the battle to loosen their tongues. That is how such commentaries reflect the excitement of the occasion.

Ski races are covered from small, secluded little boxes placed in rows at the bottom of the mountain. The commentator is not likely to see a racer in the flesh until he is within eight or ten seconds of the finishing line and even at that stage, the skier is a mere flash of colour. So men like BBC television's David Vine and ITV's Emlyn Jones rely on pictures supplied on small monitors from cameras sited at various stages of the course.

As mountains can be the most inhospitable places on which to work, it is not always possible to place a camera in difficult positions, thereby making the use of the recorded section imperative. Skiers can do many things on sections out of sight of the cameras. They can produce shattering times, disappear altogether off the side of the mountain or stumble spectacularly. But often only the clock holds the secret of the racer's fate.

That makes life most awkward for the commentator, who has to know the course, understand its tricky points and be fully aware of what is going on outside his commentary box.

Jones, a former Director General of the Sports Council, believes in skiing down the course himself before the big race of the day to get the feel of it. 'I want to know what the racers are thinking about the course and where it's most difficult. By getting out onto it myself, I can learn something about it which will be useful for the commentary,' he says. David Vine is less well known for his skiing ability, but his clear, enthusiastic commentaries and interviews provide an invaluable insight into the sport and its top competitors.

Interviews, just as much as commentating on races, can be most awkward. When Franz Klammer, or indeed any Austrian, wins on his own soil, all hell breaks loose among the crowd. Controlling such excitable supporters can make an interviewer's job a nightmare. Once Klammer was awaiting a BBC interview at the bottom of Kitzbühel's famed Hahnenkamm mountain when he was swamped by fans pushing down a wooden barrier. Suddenly, Vine found himself surrounded by hundreds of ecstatic supporters and announced somewhat grandly: 'We won't start the interview until we get all these people back.'

It was as reasonable a request as asking for Buckingham Palace to be moved a little to the left!

Vine finally got his interview, surrounded by the jostling crowd. But the episode illustrated the difficulties facing TV men in and out of their commentary booths.

Statistics

Code

Nationalities are indicated by the following symbols:

Aus	Australia	Jug	Yugoslavia	Spa	Spain
Aut	Austria	Lie	Liechtenstein	Sui	Switzerland
Bul	Bulgaria	Lux	Luxembourg	Swe	Sweden
Can	Canada	Nor	Norway	Tcn	Czechoslovakia
Fra	France	Pol	Poland	US	United States
GB	Great Britain	Sov	USSR	WG	West Germany
Ita	Italy				

Men's World championships

1966 Portillo

Downhill
1 Killy (Fra)
2 Lacroix (Fra)
3 Vogler (WG)
4 Messner (Aut)
5 Stamos (Fra)
6 Orcel (Fra)
7 Nenning (Aut)
8 Rohr (Sui)
9 Schranz (Aut)
10 Sodat (Aut)

Slalom
1 Senoner (Ita)
2 Perillat (Fra)
3 Jauffret (Fra)
4 Bogner (WG)
5 Leitner (WG)
6 Heuga (US)
7 Dibona (Ita)
8 Killy (Fra)
9 Mjön (Nor)
10 Lindström (Swe)

Giant Slalom
1 Perillat (Fra)
2 Mauduit
3 Schranz (Aut)
4 Tischhauser (Sui)
5 Killy (Fra)
6 Favre (Sui)
7 Bleiner (Aut)
8 Giovanoli (Sui)
9 Lacroix (Fra)
10 Messner (Aut)

Combination
1 Killy (Fra)
2 Lacroix (Fra)
3 Leitner (WG)

1970 Gröden

Downhill
1 Russi (Sui)
2 Cordin (Aut)
3 Milne (Aus)
4 Schranz (Aut)
5 Varallo (Ita)
6 Kidd (US)
7 Sailer (Aut)
8 Pinel (Fra)
9 Hansson (Swe)
10 Overland (Nor)

Slalom
1 Augert (Fra)
2 Russel (Fra)
3 Kidd (US)
4 Thöni (Ita)
5 Penz (Fra)
6 Giovanoli (Ita)
7 Frei (Sui)
8 Björge (Nor)
9 Ochoa (Spa)
10 Backleda (Pol)

Giant slalom
1 Schranz (Aut)
2 Bleiner (Aut)
3 Giovanoli (Sui)
4 = Messner (Aut)
   Rieger (WG)
6 Bachleda (Pol)
7 Schnider (Sui)
8 Russel (Fra)
9 Penz (Fra)
10 Haker (Nor)

Combination
1 Kidd (US)
2 Russel (Fra)
3 Backleda (Pol)

1974 St Moritz

Downhill
1 Zwilling (Aut)
2 Klammer (Aut)
3 Frommelt, W (Lie)
4 Cordin (Aut)
5 Besson (Ita)
6 Grabler (Aus)
7 Anzi (Ita)
8 Murray (Can)
9 Vesti (Sui)
10 Haker (Nor)

Slalom
1 Thöni (Ita)
2 Zwilling (Aut)
3 Ochoa (Spa)
4 Bonnevie (Fra)
5 Tresch (Sui)
6 Söderin (Swe)
7 Backleda (Pol)
8 Junginger (WG)
9 Barroso (Fra)
10 Goodman (Can)

Giant slalom
1 Thöni (Ita)
2 Hinterseer (Aut)
3 Gros (Ita)
4 Schmalzl (Ita)
5 Pargätzi (Sui)
6 Stricker (Ita)
7 Pechtl (Aut)
8 Rieger (WG)
9 Stenmark (Swe)
10 Klammer (Aut)

Combination
1 Klammer (Aut)
2 Backleda (Pol)
3 Junginger (WG)

1978 Garmisch

Downhill
1 Walcher (Aut)
2 Veith (WG)
3 Grissmann (Aut)
4 Ferstl (WG)
5 Klammer (Aut)
   Müller (Sui)
7 Podborski (Can)
8 Vesti (Sui)
9 Makeev (Sov)
10 Plank (Ita)

Slalom
1 Stenmark (Swe)
2 Gros (Ita)
3 Frommelt, P (Lie)
4 Steriner (Aut)
5 Bernardi (Ita)
6 Neureuther (WG)
7 Kaiwa (Jpn)
8 Mahre, S (US)
9 Jakobsson (Swe)
10 Aellig (Sui)

Giant slalom
1 Stenmark (Swe)
2 Wenzel (Lie)
3 Frommelt, W (Lie)
4 Hemmi (Sui)
5 Mahre, P (US)
6 Enn (Aut)
7 Lüscher (Sui)
8 Patterson (US)
9 Adgate (US)
10 Nöckler (Ita)

Combination
1 Wenzel (Lie)
2 Ferstl (WG)
3 Patterson (US)

1982 Schladming

Downhill
1. Weirather (Aut)
2. Cathomen (Sui)
3. Resch (Aut)
4. Heinzer (Sui)
5. Müller (Sui)
6. Makeev (Sov)
7. Klammer (Aut)
8. Bürgler (Sui)
9. Podborski (Can)
10. Mair (Ita)

Slalom
1. Stenmark (Swe)
2. Krizaj (Jug)
3. Fjaellberg (Swe)
4. De Chiesa (Ita)
5. Gaspoz (Sui)
6. Gros (Ita)
7. Mally (Ita)
8. Gruber (Aut)
9. Skajem (Nor)
10. Andreev (Sov)

Giant Slalom
1. Mahre, S (US)
2. Stenmark (Swe)
3. Strel (Jug)
4. Gaspoz (Sui)
5. Nöckler (Ita)
6. Enn (Aut)
7. Krizaj (Jug)
8. Fournier (Sui)
9. Navillod (Fra)
10. Strolz (Aut)

Combination
1. Vion (Fra)
2. Lüscher (Sui)
3. Steiner (Aut)

Men's World cup points

Overall

1974	pts	1975	pts
1 Gros (Ita)	181	1 Thöni (Ita)	250
2 Thöni (Ita)	165	2 Stenmark (Swe)	245
3 Hinterseer (Aut)	162	3 Klammer (Aut)	240
4 Collombin (Sui)	140	4 Gros (Ita)	196
5 Klammer (Aut)	125	5 Haker (Nor)	147
6 Stricker (Ita)	98	6 Hinterseer (Aut)	117
1976		**1977**	
1 Stenmark (Swe)	249	1 Stenmark (Swe)	339
2 Gros (Ita)	205	2 Heidegger (Aut)	250
3 Thöni (Ita)	190	3 Klammer (Aut)	165
4 Klammer (Aut)	181	4 Gros (Ita)	165
5 Hinterseer (Aut)	98	5 Russi (Sui)	148
6 Tresch (Sui)	98	6 Thöni (Ita)	145
1978		**1979**	
1 Stenmark (Swe)	150	1 Lüscher (Sui)	186
2 Mahre, P (US)	116	2 Stock (Aut)	163
3 Wenzel, A (Lie)	100	3 Mahre, P (US)	155
4 Heidegger (Aut)	95	4 Gros (Ita)	152
5 =Klammer (Aut)	70	5 Stenmark (Swe)	150
Plank (Ita)	70	6 Wenzel A. (Lie)	148

1980		1981	
1 Wenzel A. (Lie)	204	1 Mahre, P (US)	266
2 Stenmark (Swe)	200	2 Stenmark (Swe)	260
3 Mahre, P (US)	132	3 Zhirov (Sov)	185
4 Krizaj (Jug)	131	4 Mahre, S (US)	155
5 Steiner (Aut)	130	5 Müller (Sui)	140
6 Lüthy (Sui)	116	6 Krizaj (Jug)	137
1982		**1983**	
1 Mahre, P (US)	309	1 Mahre, P (US)	285
2 Stenmark (Swe)	211	2 Stenmark (Swe)	218
3 Mahre, S (US)	183	3 Wenzel, A (Lie)	177
4 Müller (Sui)	132	4 Girardelli (Lux)	168
5 Wenzel, A (Lie)	129	5 Lüscher (Sui)	164
6 Girardelli (Lux)	121	6 Zurbriggen (Sui)	161

Downhill

1980	pts	1981	pts
1 Müller (Sui)	96	1 Weirather (Aut)	115
2 Read (Can)	87	2 Podborski (Can)	110
3 Plank (Ita)	81	3 Müller (Sui)	95
4 Weirather (Aut)	75	4 Wirnsberger (Aut)	73
5 Haker (Nor)	64	5 Spiess (Aut)	56
6 Wirnsberger (Aut)	63	6 =Tsyganov (Sov)	55
		Bürgler (Sui)	55
1982		**1983**	
1 =Podborski (Can)	115	1 Klammer (Aut)	95
Müller (Sui)	115	2 Cathomen (Sui)	92
3 Weirather (Aut)	97	3 Weirather (Aut)	74
4 Resch (Aut)	76	4 Resch (Sui)	73
5 Klammer (Aut)	71	5 =Lüscher (Sui)	72
6 Reed (Can)	65	Raeber (Sui)	72

Slalom

1980		1981	
1 Sternmark (Swe)	125	1 Stenmark (Swe)	120
2 Krizaj (Jug)	88	2 Mahre, P (USA)	97
3 Neureuther (WG)	69	3 =Krizaj (Jug)	80
4 Popangelov (Bul)	64	Mahre, S (US)	80
5 Zhirov (Sov)	57	5 Frommelt (Lie)	77
6 Orlainsky (Aut)	55	6 Zhirov (Sov)	70
1982		**1983**	
1 Mahre, P (US)	120	1 Stenmark (Swe)	110
2 Stenmark (Swe)	110	2 Strand (Swe)	110
3 Mahre, S (US)	92	3 Wenzel, A (Lie)	92
4 De Chiesa (Ita)	68	4 Mahre, S (US)	80
5 Gruber (Aut)	66	5 Krizaj (Jug)	78
6 Krizaj (Jug)	63	6 Mahre, P (US)	75

Giant slalom

1980	pts	1981	pts
1 Stenmark (Swe)	125	1 Stenmark (Swe)	125
2 Enn (Aut)	87	2 Zhirov (Sov)	115
3 Lüthy (Sui)	82	3 Mahre, P (US)	84
4 Wenzel, A (Lie)	71	4 Gaspoz (Sui)	71
5 Gaspoz (Sui)	68	5 Fournier (Sui)	62
6 Krizaj (Jug)	56	6 Orlainsky (Aut)	61

1982		1983	
1 Mahre, P (US)	105	1 Mahre, P (US)	107
2 Stenmark (Swe)	101	2 Stenmark (Swe)	100
3 Girardelli (Lux)	77	3 Julen (Swe)	100
4 Enn (Aut)	75	4 Zurbriggen (Sui)	90
5 Gaspoz (Sui)	70	5 Enn (Aut)	83
6 Zurbriggen (Sui)	67	6 Girardelli (Lux)	52

Women's world championships

1970 Gröden	**1974 St Moritz**	**1978 Garmisch**	**1982 Schladming**
Downhill	*Downhill*	*Downhill*	*Downhill*
1 Zyrd (Sui)	1 Moser-Pröll (Aut)	1 Moser-Pröll (Aut)	1 Sorensen (Can)
2 Mir (Fra)	2 Clifford (Can)	2 Epple, I (WG)	2 Nelson (US)
3 Moser-Pröll (Aut)	3 Drexel (Aut)	3 De Agostini (Sui)	3 Graham (Can)
4 Crawford (Can)	4 Kaserer (Aut)	4 Nadig (Sui)	4 Fjelstad (Nor)
5 Gfölner (Aut)	5 Nadig (Sui)	5 Nelson (US)	5 Lehodey (Can)
6 Steurer (Fra)	6 Tisot (Ita)	6 Mittermaier (WG)	6 Kirchler (Aut)
7 Hafen (WG)	7 Kreiner (Can)	7 Habersatter (Aut)	7 De Agostini (Sui)
8 Jacot (Fra)	8 Förland (Nor)	8 Ellmer (Aut)	8 Epple, I (WG)
9 Cochran, M (US)	9 Crawford (Can)	9 Lukasser (Aut)	9 Flanders (US)
10 Christiansen (Nor)	10 Serrat (Fra)	10 Bader (WG)	10 Oak (US)
Slalom	*Slalom*	*Slalom*	*Slalom*
1 Lafforgue (Fra)	1 Wenzel, H (Lie)	1 Sölkner (Aut)	1 Hess (Sui)
2 Cochran, B (US)	2 Jacot (Fra)	2 Behr (WG)	2 Cooper (US)
3 Jacot (Fra)	3 Morerod (Sui)	3 Kaserer (Aut)	3 Zini (Ita)
4 Gabl (Aut)	4 Serrat (Fra)	4 Pelen (Fra)	4 Tlalka (Pol)
5 Nagel (US)	5 Giordani (Ita)	5 Serrat (Fra)	5 Quario (Ita)
6 Cochran, M (US)	6 Mittermaier (WG)	6 Wenzel, H (Lie)	6 Epple, M (WG)
7 Steurer (Fra)	7 Kaserer (Aus)	7 Morerod (Sui)	7 Steiner (Aut)
8 Clifford (Can)	8 Förland (Nor)	8 Giordani (Ita)	8 Jerman (JUG)
9 Rauter (Aut)	9 Puig (Spa)	9 Zeichmeister (WG)	9 Charvatova (Tch)
10 Hathorn (GB)	10 Behr (WG)	10 Mösenlechner (WG)	10 Serrat (Fra)
Giant slalom	*Giant slalom*	*Giant slalom*	*Giant Slalom*
1 Clifford (Can)	1 Serrat (Fra)	1 Epple, M (WG)	1 Hess (Sui)
2 Lafforgue (Fra)	2 Treichl (WG)	2 Morerod (Sui)	2 Cooper (US)
3 Macchi (Fra)	3 Rouvier (Fra)	3 Moser-Pröll (Aut)	3 Konzett (Lie)
4 Jacot (Fra)	4 Moser-Pröll (Aut)	4 Epple, I (WG)	4 Wenzel, P (Lie)
5 Gabl (Aut)	5 Kaserer (Aut)	5 Wenzel, H (Lie)	5 Serrat (Fra)
6 Cochran, M (US)	6 Cochran, B (US)	6 Serrat (Fra)	6 McKinney (US)
7 Mittermaier (WG)	7 Wenzel, H (Lie)	7 Konzett (Lie)	7 Zini (Ita)
8 Steurer (Fra)	8 Cochran, M (US)	8 Pelen (Fra)	8 Kirchler (Aut)
9 Cochran, B (US)	9 Crawford (Can)	9 Hess (Sui)	9 Kinshofer (WG)
10 Galica (GB)	10 Kerscher (Aut)	10 Zechmeister (WG)	10 Steiner (Aut)
Combination	*Combination*	*Combination*	*Combination*
1 Jacot (Fra)	1 Serrat (Fra)	1 Moser-Pröll (Aut)	1 Hess (Sui)
2 Steurer (Fra)	2 Wenzel, H (Lie)	2 Wenzel, H (Lie)	2 Pelen (Fra)
3 Cochran, M (US)	3 Kaserer (Aut)	3 Serrat (Fra)	3 Cooper (US)

Women's World cup points

1974	pts	1975	pts
1 Moser-Pröll (Aut)	268	1 Moser-Pröll (Aut)	305
2 Kaserer (Aut)	153	2 Wenzel, H (Lie)	199
3 Wenzel, H (Lie)	144	3 Mittermaier (WG)	166
4 Zechmeister (WG)	129	4 Nadig (Sui)	154
5 Serrat (Fra)	127	5 =Serrat (Fra)	153
6 Nadig (Sui)	123	Zurbriggen (Sui)	153

1976		1977	
1 Mittermaier (WG)	281	1 Morerod (Sui)	319
2 Morerod (Sui)	214	2 Moser-Pröll (Aut)	246
3 Kaserer (Aut)	171	3 Kaserer (Aut)	196
4 Zurbriggen (Sui)	170	4 Habersatter (Aut)	186
5 Debernard (Fra)	164	5 Wenzel, H (Lie)	150
6 Totschnig (Aut)	155	6 Nadig (Sui)	133

1978		1979	
1 Wenzel, H (Lie)	154	1 Moser-Pröll (Aut)	243
2 Moser-Pröll (Aut)	147	2 Wenzel, H (Lie)	240
3 Morerod (Sui)	135	3 Epple, I (WG)	189
4 Serrat (Fra)	105	4 Nelson (US)	168
5 Nelson (US)	97	5 Nadig (Sui)	156
6 Pelen (Fra)	96	6 Serrat (Fra)	151

1980		1981	
1 Wenzel H. (Lie)	311	1 Nadig (Sui)	289
2 Moser-Pröll (Aut)	259	2 Hess (Sui)	251
3 Nadig (Sui)	221	3 Wenzel, H (Lie)	241
4 Pelen (Fra)	192	4 Cooper (US)	198
5 Epple, I (WG)	141	5 Epple, I (WG)	181
6 Serrat (Fra)	124	6 McKinney (US)	176

1982		1983	
1 Hess (Sui)	297	1 McKinney (US)	225
2 Epple, I (WG)	282	2 Wenzel, H (Lie)	193
3 Cooper (US)	198	3 Hess (Sui)	192
4 Epple, M (WG)	166	4 Kirchler (Aut)	163
5 Nelson (US)	158	5 Walliser (Sui)	135
6 =Sölkner (Aut)	137	6 Epple, I (WG)	117
Konzett (Lie)	137		

Downhill

1980	pts	1981	pts
1 Nadig (Sui)	125	1 Nadig (Sui)	120
2 Moser-Pröll (Aut)	100	2 De Agostini (Sui)	110
3 Wenzel, H (Lie)	66	3 Moser-Pröll (Aut)	78
4 Nelson (US)	59	4 Epple, I (WG)	71
5 Soltysova (Tch)	58	5 Fjeldstad (Nor)	62
6 Epple, I (WG)	51	6 Soltysova (Tch)	61
1982		**1983**	
1 Gros-Gaudenier (Fra)	87	1 De Agostini (Sui)	106
2 =Flanders (US)	84	2 Walliser (Sui)	97
De Agostini (Sui)	84	3 Kirchler (Aut)	76
4 Sorensen (Can)	81		
5 Epple, I (WG)	69		
6 Sölkner (Aut)	64		

Slalom

1980		1981	
1 Pelen (Fra)	120	1 Hess (Sui)	125
2 Wenzel, H (Lie)	100	2 Cooper (US)	86
3 Moser-Pröll (Aut)	88	3 =Zini (Ita)	81
4 Zini (Ita)	78	Pelen (Fra)	81
5 Giordani (Ita)	75	5 Serrat (Fra)	63
6 Hess (Sui)	62	6 Wenzel, H (Lie)	59
1982		**1983**	
1 Hess (Sui)	125	1 Hess (Sui)	110
2 Konzett (Lie)	100	2 McKinney (US)	105
3 Cooper (US)	83	3 Quario (Ita)	89
4 Quario (Ita)	67	4 Wenzel, H (Lie)	82
5 Pelen (Fra)	67	5 Steiner (Aut)	70
6 Zini (Fra)	66	6 Kronbichler (Aut)	66

Giant slalom

1980	pts	1981	pts
1 Wenzel, H (Lie)	125	1 McKinney (US)	102
2 =Pelen (Fra)	95	2 Nadig (Sui)	95
Nadig (Sui)	95	3 =Hess (Sui)	78
4 Epple, I (WG)	83	Wenzel, H (Lie)	78
5 Hess (Sui)	71	Epple, I (WG)	78
6 Serrat (Fra)	55	6 Epple, M (WG)	71
1982		**1983**	
1 Epple, I (WG)	120	1 McKinney (US)	120
2 Epple, M (WG)	110	2 Nelson (US)	83
3 Hess (Sui)	105	3 Epple, M (WG)	81
4 McKinney (US)	74	4 Hess (Sui)	78
5 Cooper (US)	68	5 Wenzel, H (Lie)	77
6 Pelen (Fra)	48	6 Serrat (Fra)	68

Acknowledgements

We are most grateful to the Ski Club of Great Britain, David Vine, Harti Weirather, Phil Mahre and Franz Klammer, whose help and advice have been invaluable. Other suggested reading: *Ski Sunday* John Samuel (BBC Publications).

Additional photographs by Associated Press (pages, 17, 21, 27, 31, 39, 46); George Koenig (11, 22).

Cross-country skiing in Norway.